COAST 2 COAST 2 COAST

INDIGENOUS LIFE IN CANADA: PAST, PRESENT, FUTURE

STEWARDSHIP

BY ANITA YASUDA

CONTENT CONSULTANT

M. A. SMITH, PHD, ASSOCIATE
PROFESSOR, NATURAL RESOURCES
MANAGEMENT, LAKEHEAD UNIVERSITY

Coast2Coast2Coast is published by Beech Street Books
27 Stewart Rd. Collingwood, ON Canada L9Y 4M7

www.beechstreetbooks.ca

Produced by Red Line Editorial

Photographs ©: Chris Cheadle/All Canada Photos/Glow Images, cover, 1; NativeStock/North Wind Picture Archives, 4–5, 26–27; Nancy Carter/North Wind Picture Archives, 7; Mary Evans Picture Library/Alamy, 8–9; Duncan Campbell Scott/Library and Archives Canada/PA-059592, 11; SandyS/ Shutterstock Images, 12–13; Red Line Editorial, 14, 20; Tanya Talaga/ ZumaPress/Newscom, 16–17; Heinz Ruckemann/UPI/Newscom, 19; Keith Beaty/Toronto Star/ZumaPress/Newscom, 22–23; Spencer Robertson/ Newscom, 29

Editor: Marie Pearson
Designer: Nikki Farinella

Library and Archives Canada Cataloguing in Publication

Yasuda, Anita, author
        Stewardship / by Anita Yasuda.

(Indigenous life in Canada : past, present, future)
Includes bibliographical references and index.
Issued in print and electronic formats.
ISBN 978-1-77308-121-2 (hardcover).--ISBN 978-1-77308-181-6 (softcover).--
ISBN 978-1-77308-241-7 (PDF).--ISBN 978-1-77308-280-6 (HTML)

        1. Traditional ecological knowledge--Canada--Juvenile literature.
2. Native peoples--Ecology--Canada--Juvenile literature. 3. Environmental management--Canada--Juvenile literature. I. Title.

E78.C2Y37 2017   j304.2089'97071   C2017-903015-9
                                                 C2017-903016-7

Printed in the United States of America
Mankato, MN
August 2017

TABLE OF CONTENTS

LAND AND CULTURES

For centuries Indigenous Peoples have lived across the geographically diverse region now known as Canada. They lived in regions Canada today calls the Arctic, Subarctic, Northwest Coast, Plateau, Plains, and Eastern Woodlands. The unique qualities of each region influence the lives of the Indigenous Peoples who have lived there for countless generations. They learned how to responsibly use and take care of the land. This is called **stewardship**.

Indigenous Peoples learned how life worked within their territories. They studied animals and plants. They

First Nations such as the Cree used many parts of the animals they hunted, including making bear claws into necklaces.

learned in which season certain plants would grow. They knew when fish would **migrate** from the ocean to the rivers. They used these skills to know when they could hunt, trap, or gather. Stewardship of the land was important. They were careful to take only what they needed from the land. And they gave thanks to the Creator, a spirit who made the world and gave people these gifts.

Agriculture

Long before Europeans arrived, the Huron-Wendat knew how to survive in their environment. The men hunted. The women raised crops on the land by Georgian Bay and Lake

GREAT MOTHER AATAENTSIC

Many **cultures** tell creation stories to explain their world. One such story told by the Huron-Wendat explains the close link between the people and their land. It tells of the woman Aataentsic. She falls through a hole in the sky. Animals come to help the woman. They use mud to create land on a turtle's shell. The woman walks over the land, planting corn, beans, and squash from her world. These plants become the crops that the Huron-Wendat grow.

The three sisters, corn, beans, and squash, grow in a garden mound.

Simcoe. In the spring, they built small mounds over the land. They planted three types of seeds in each mound. These seeds were corn, beans, and squash. The Huron-Wendat called the plants "the three sisters" because they helped each other grow. Beans climbed up the tall corn stems. The roots of the bean plants put **nutrients** in the soil. The squash vines kept the weeds away. The Huron-Wendat worked the same fields until the soil's nutrients were used up. Then they moved to new land and began again.

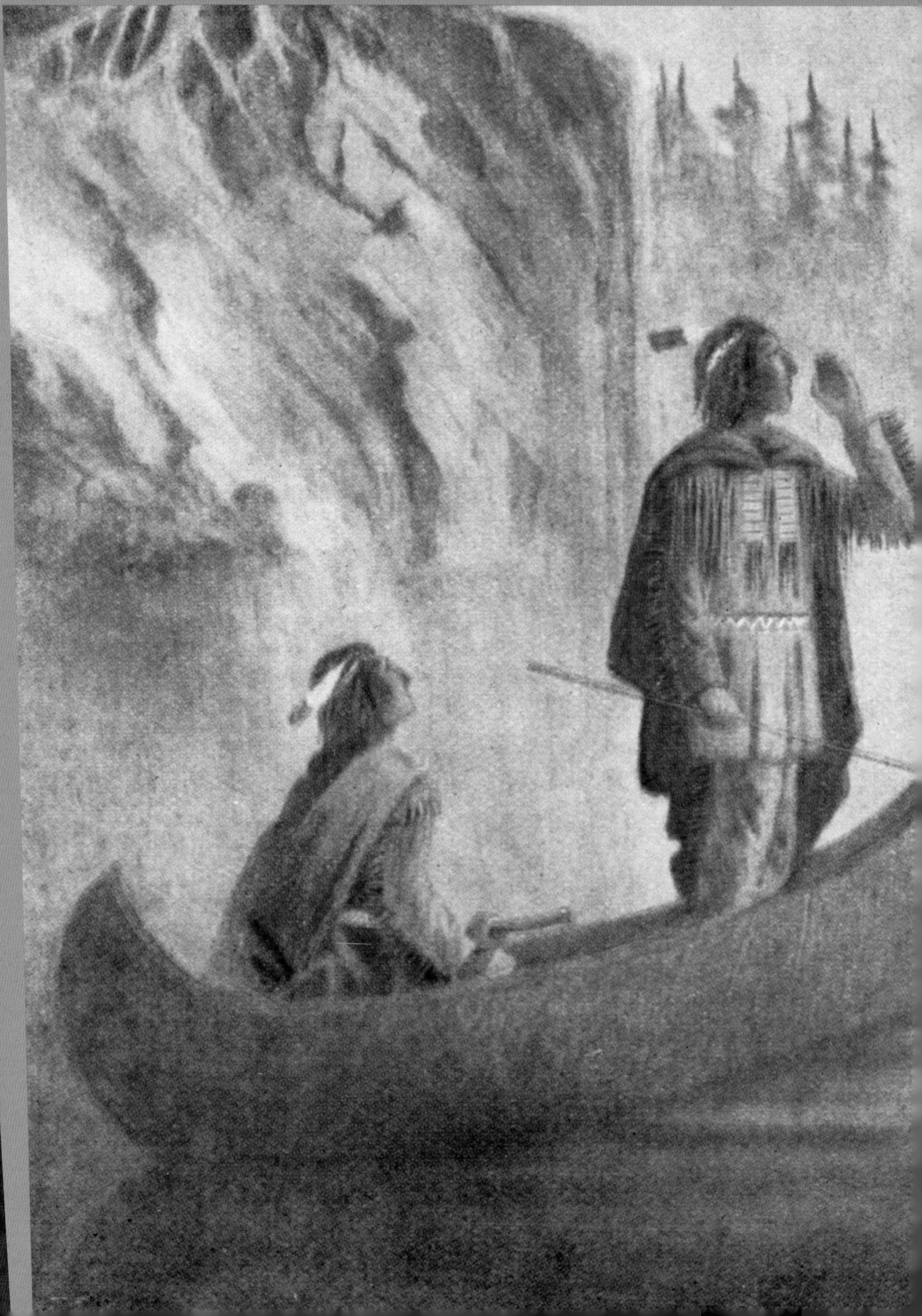

CHANGE AND CHALLENGES

The Algonquins lived in small family communities. Their lands had many natural resources. They hunted and fished across the eastern Great Lakes region. During the warmer months, Algonquins gathered wild plants. They planted small gardens.

European traders arrived in Canada in the 1500s. Their arrival preceded the coming of many more Europeans. In the early 1600s the French set up a colony by the St. Lawrence River. The Algonquins shared their knowledge of the land with the French. They traded beaver pelts. In exchange they received goods such as

An artist imagines two Algonquin men in a canoe.

clothing, iron tools, and, later, guns. In time the fur trade grew. Soon animals such as beavers became scarce because of over-trapping. This led to wars, sometimes called the Beaver Wars, between Indigenous communities as they fought for control over land where beavers still lived.

Damaging Connections to the Land

In 1876 the Canadian government passed the Indian Act. Under the Act, First Nations did not have the same rights as other Canadians. The Act and historic **treaties** stripped First Nations' control of their resources. Indigenous children were taken away from their homes. Generations of people grew up never knowing their families, lands, or cultures.

As more Europeans came, they made treaties to gain farmland from Indigenous Peoples. The treaties pushed First Nations into smaller areas. In 1929 the Cree and Ojibwe wanted to protect their land, which was being drained of its resources by trappers. They approached the

Two Ojibwe women attend the payment ceremony for Treaty 9.

government to make a treaty. The government did not let them negotiate treaty terms. The Nations signed Treaty 9, or the James Bay Treaty, and the government measured out 2.6 square kilometres of land per family of five. This land was called a **reserve**. Many First Nations now prefer the term First Nation community and no longer use reserve. Reserves disrupted their ways of life and economies. They were too small to hold enough resources to support a Nation.

LAND RIGHTS AND MANAGING THE LAND

oday some Indigenous Peoples negotiate land claims with the Canadian government. Most of these claims are raised by Indigenous nations who do not have a treaty with the Government of Canada. In 1998 the Nisga'a settled their claim for land with the Government of British Columbia and the Government of Canada. It was the first modern-day treaty in the province. Under the Nisga'a Treaty, the Nisga'a own and manage about 2,000 square

The Nisga'a work to preserve the natural resources and beauty of their land, including Lava Lake.

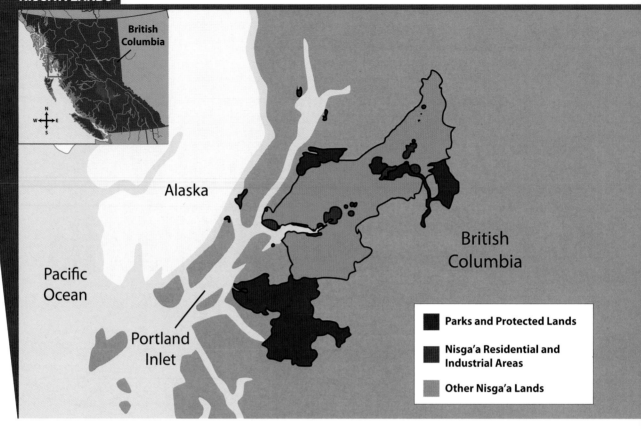

British Columbia

Alaska

British Columbia

Pacific Ocean

Portland Inlet

Parks and Protected Lands

Nisga'a Residential and Industrial Areas

Other Nisga'a Lands

kilometres of land in the Nass River Valley. That is only 5 percent of their traditional territory.

The river valley has always been rich in resources. The mountains, lakes, and rivers hold many types of plants and animals. The Nisga'a are known for their stewardship of the Nass River. They keep track of fish **species**. They note their size. They keep records on salmon levels. Their efforts ensure that these resources will be here for people in the future.

Land-Use Plans

The First Nations, Inuit, and Métis Peoples believe they have a responsibility to care for the land. Some First Nations work together to do this. In 2002 four Anishinaabe Nations signed an agreement to work as a team. They were the Poplar River, Little Grand Rapids, Pauingassi, and Pikangikum First Nations. A portion of their lands covers large areas of **boreal** forest in Manitoba and Ontario.

The Nations want to manage their lands using traditional Anishinaabe values and knowledge. So each Nation made a land-use plan. A land-use plan is a tool that looks at how a Nation has used its lands and waters in the past. Plans also study possible new uses. The Nations used their plans to set aside an area of the boreal forest to be protected. The area is called Pimachiowin Aki. These words mean "the land that gives life." In 2017 they asked the United Nations to make Pimachiowin Aki a World Heritage Site. This would protect the area into the future.

CHAPTER FOUR

PROTECTING TRADITIONAL RESOURCES

Water is important to all life. Water has always been honoured by the First Nations, Métis, and Inuit. In many Indigenous communities, mainly the women have the responsibility to look after the water. It is a part of Indigenous stories. It is used in **ceremonies** to cleanse and heal. Yet in 2016, 90 First Nation communities did not have access to clean or safe drinking water.

Children in the Neskantaga First Nation of northwestern Ontario have never had access to clean tap water. In 1995

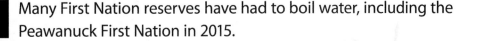

Many First Nation reserves have had to boil water, including the Peawanuck First Nation in 2015.

the Neskantaga water plant broke down. Since then the community has had to boil water to make it safe to drink. People must go to the plant to pick up bottles of water. This is not easy for elderly people or families. In 2013 the Government of Canada passed a bill to make sure that all First Nations have safe drinking water. In 2014 the government said that it would build a new water plant for the Neskantaga First Nation community, but the money for the project would not be available until 2017.

Fighting Pipelines

Nations such as the Kanesatake Mohawk work to keep water resources

RENEWABLE ENERGY

The sun's energy is powerful. It can be used to heat homes or make electricity. The Louis Bull First Nation is in Alberta. In 2013 its members wanted to look at ways they could live in balance with nature. So they began collecting the sun's energy with solar panels. The panels change the energy into electricity. The sun is a source of renewable energy that will never run out. As of 2016 the community had 400 solar panels. The panels power buildings such as a training centre and fire hall.

First Nations members protest the Northern Gateway Pipeline.

pure. Pipelines carry oil from an oil well through pipes
that usually run under the ground. In 2016 the Kanesatake
joined with more than 50 other Indigenous Nations
in North America. The Nations signed a treaty to stop

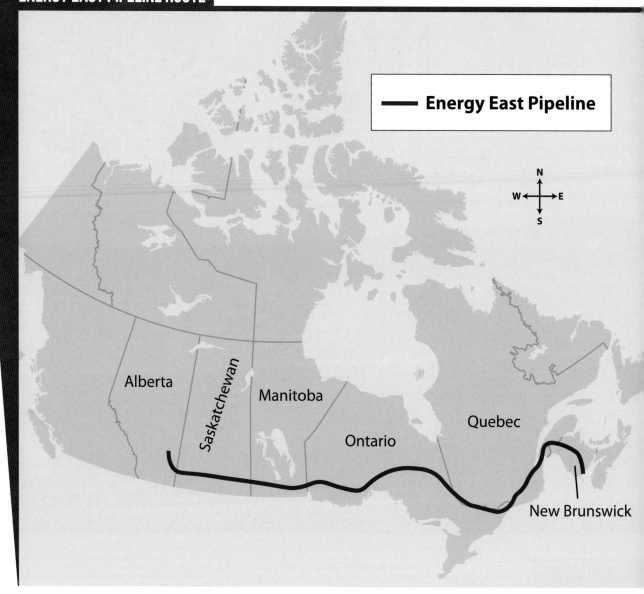

pipelines on their lands. They believe that a spill could

harm important resources such as water.

One pipeline the Kanesatake are protesting is the

Energy East pipeline. If it is built, it would run from Alberta to New Brunswick. It would carry about 1.1 million barrels of oil every day. This is enough oil to fill approximately 70 Olympic-sized swimming pools. A part of the pipeline would cross the Ottawa River. The Kanesatake have always fished and hunted here. If oil spilled, it would poison the water, harming both people and animals.

Indigenous people work to raise awareness about water pollution in other ways, too. The Great Lakes provide drinking water to over 30 million people. But the lakes are threatened by pollution. Josephine Mandamin, an Anishinaabe elder, and other Anishinaabe people have been leading Water Walks around the Great Lakes. They walked around Lake Superior in 2003, Lake Michigan in 2004, Lake Huron in 2005, Lake Ontario in 2006, and Lake Erie in 2007. Since then they have walked other lakes and rivers. They hope these walks help people realize how important water is and that it needs protecting.

CHAPTER FIVE

CULTURALLY IMPORTANT RESOURCES TODAY

Many cultures have origin stories that tell of gifts. Long ago the Anishinaabe people lived by the Atlantic Ocean. Their origin stories tell that they moved west to find food that grew on the water. That food was wild rice.

Airboats have flat bottoms, so they skim over the surface of the water, knocking rice into a tray at the front of the boat.

Some Anishinaabe Nations still care for wild rice. It is an important part of preserving their culture. Northern Ontario is home to the Wabigoon Lake Ojibway Nation. The Nation opened its wild rice plant in 1988. Workers do not harvest wild rice with canoes and poles as was done in the past. They use modern equipment such as small, open airboats. First Nations youth in the area also learn about the harvest. Students are taught how to map traditional rice-harvesting areas.

Rights and Forgiveness

Until 100 years ago the Champagne and Aishihik First Nations and Kluane First Nation relied on the land for food. They hunted animals such as sheep or caribou in what is now Yukon. They trapped and fished. In 1943 the federal government created a protected wildlife area on their lands. But the government banned the First Nations from using the land. The ban ended in 1976. But the First Nations did not return right away. They did not trust the government. They worried that their rights to hunt or fish might be taken away again.

In 2004 Parks Canada began the Healing Broken Connections Project to bring First Nations people back to their lands that are now part of parks. In 2007 elders of the Champagne and Aishihik First Nations and the Kluane First Nation forgave Parks Canada in the Kluane National Park and Reserve. At the week-long camp, elders and park rangers took part in traditional activities. They fished and hunted together. Elders told stories of the area. Today First Nations' knowledge of the land is used to manage the park.

REINTRODUCING BISON

Bison have always been important to the Siksika. They once hunted this large mammal on grasslands that are now part of Alberta. The hunt was an important part of their beliefs. The people ate the bison's meat. They used the hide for clothing and the bones for tools. In 2015 the Siksika signed the Buffalo Treaty. The agreement was signed by First Nations in Canada and the United States. They hoped to bring bison back to the land. In 2017 bison returned to Banff National Park.

CHAPTER SIX

STEWARDSHIP AND THE FUTURE

Many Indigenous Peoples practise their traditional ideas of caring for the land through stewardship programs that look after plant diversity or cultural sites such as ancient fishing villages. There are about 30 programs in Canada. In 2016 Indigenous leaders put forward a plan. They wanted to create a new stewardship program. It would build on the work of these other programs. Eventually it would span the country.

The Haida of Haida Gwaii run the oldest stewardship program in the country. It began in 1973. They track wildlife populations and take care of their lands. The Innu

This Seneca nursery owner grows and sells native plants to preserve them and help improve ecosystems.

in Labrador also manage their lands. They work in areas such as forestry. Another program is the Coastal Guardian Watchmen Network. The K'ómoks First Nation is a member. The Nation runs studies and maps plants. The Nation's researchers use this information to clean up the habitat of fish such as salmon. They restore shoreline and grow plants to reduce erosion along the stream. Because of their work, the waters where fish feed and grow in the K'ómoks Estuary are healthier.

In 2017 the Government of Canada set aside $25 million to give to Indigenous Guardian programs over five years. Indigenous guardians help the Government of

HEALTHY LANDS

The Wahnapitae First Nation in Ontario is looking at ways to keep all living things in its area healthy. One area of focus is biodiversity. This means having many kinds of plants and animals on their lands. The Nation is working with the city of Sudbury to map invasive species. These are species that are unwanted. They destroy native plants and animals.

The Haida Guardian Watchmen protect the land at Haida cultural sites on Haida Gwaii.

Canada with conservation. They take care of the land and its resources.

Youth and Stewardship

More than half of all First Nations, Métis, and Inuit people call cities home. For some youth this can make it harder to learn their history. Many communities are helping their young people reconnect to the land. The Lutsel K'e Dene First Nation is in the Northwest Territories. It runs a program called the Ni Hat'ni Dene. This means Dene "watchers of the land." It pairs young people with older members of the community. In the summer, youth gain skills needed to care for the environment. They test water and take samples of fish. They learn how to live off the land. The program is a way for them to take pride in their culture.

GLOSSARY

BOREAL
northern areas that usually have forests of evergreen plants

CEREMONIES
formal events that hold social and spiritual significance and are celebrated by many people

CULTURES
the beliefs and customs of groups of people

MIGRATE
when a group of animals moves from place to place

NUTRIENTS
substances needed for a living thing to survive

RESERVE
an area of land set apart by the federal government for the use and benefit of a First Nation and where Indigenous people can choose to live

SPECIES
a class of living organisms that have some characteristics in common

STEWARDSHIP
the responsible use and protection of the land, animals, plants, and air

TREATIES
agreements between two or more groups of people

TO LEARN MORE

BOOKS

Isaac, Michael James. *The Lost Teachings/Panuijkatasikl Kina'masuti'l*. Winnipeg, Manitoba: Roseway, 2013.

Jones, Molly. *Relationships with Aboriginal First Nations*. Collingwood, Ontario: Beech Street Books, 2017.

Silvey, Diane. *The Kids Book of Aboriginal Peoples in Canada*. Toronto, Ontario: Kids Can Press, 2012.

WEBSITES

Journeys & Transformations: British Columbia Landscapes
http://www.virtualmuseum.ca/virtual-exhibits/exhibit/journeys-transformations-british-columbia-landscapes

CBC News: Bison Reintroduced to Banff National Park: Video
http://www.cbc.ca/news/canada/calgary/bison-buffalo-banff-national-park-1.3969106

TNC Canada: Indigenous Stewardship
http://www.tnccanada.ca/our-work/themes/canada-indigenous-stewardship.xml

INDEX

ABOUT THE AUTHOR

Anita Yasuda is the author of many children's books. Anita was born in Canada and grew up in southern Ontario. She graduated from the University of Toronto before pursuing teaching in Asia and in British Columbia. She divides her time between both coasts, where you can find her on most days walking her dog and thinking of more stories to write. She enjoys writing biographies, books about science and social studies, and chapter books.